YOUR KNOWLEDGE HAS VALUE

- We will publish your bachelor's and master's thesis, essays and papers

- Your own eBook and book - sold worldwide in all relevant shops

- Earn money with each sale

Upload your text at www.GRIN.com
and publish for free

Bibliographic information published by the German National Library:

The German National Library lists this publication in the National Bibliography; detailed bibliographic data are available on the Internet at http://dnb.dnb.de .

This book is copyright material and must not be copied, reproduced, transferred, distributed, leased, licensed or publicly performed or used in any way except as specifically permitted in writing by the publishers, as allowed under the terms and conditions under which it was purchased or as strictly permitted by applicable copyright law. Any unauthorized distribution or use of this text may be a direct infringement of the author s and publisher s rights and those responsible may be liable in law accordingly.

Imprint:

Copyright © 2017 GRIN Verlag, Open Publishing GmbH
Print and binding: Books on Demand GmbH, Norderstedt Germany
ISBN: 9783668511248

This book at GRIN:

http://www.grin.com/en/e-book/373562/scenarios-and-their-application-in-future-oriented-research

Felix Zappe

Scenarios and their application in future oriented research

An analysis of the value and limitations of the use of scenario techniques

GRIN Publishing

GRIN - Your knowledge has value

Since its foundation in 1998, GRIN has specialized in publishing academic texts by students, college teachers and other academics as e-book and printed book. The website www.grin.com is an ideal platform for presenting term papers, final papers, scientific essays, dissertations and specialist books.

Visit us on the internet:

http://www.grin.com/

http://www.facebook.com/grincom

http://www.twitter.com/grin_com

Scenarios and their application in future-oriented research

An analysis of the value and limitations of the use of scenario techniques

Individual assignment as part of assessment for the study unit
Foresight Techniques for Creativity & Innovation – IOT 5007

Handed in by:
Felix Zappe

Written at the Edward de Bono Institute

University of Malta

Msida, June 2017

Content

TABLES AND FIGURES II

1   INTRODUCTION TO THE SCENARIO TECHNIQUE 1

2   ADVANTAGES AND DISADVANTAGES OF SCENARIOS 3

3   REFLECTIONS ON OUR SCENARIO TECHNIQUE APPLICATION DURING OUR FORESIGHT STUDY .. 5

REFERENCES IV

Tables and figures

FIGURE 1: KEY PROCESS STEPS OF SCENARIO ANALYSES (SOURCE: KOSOW AND GASSNER, 2008, P. 25). 1

FIGURE 2: CHARACTERISTICS OF QUALITATIVE VS. QUANTITATIVE AND EXPLORATIVE VS. NORMATIVE SCENARIOS (SOURCE: KOSOW AND GASSNER, 2008, PP. 32-34). 3

FIGURE 3: OVERVIEW OF DIFFERENT SCENARIO TECHNIQUE APPROACHES (SOURCE: KOSOW AND GASSNER, 2008, PP. 76-77)............ 6

1 Introduction to the Scenario Technique

Kosow and Gassner (2008) propose in their comprehensive study of scenario techniques, their application and theoretical foundations some basic characteristics of scenario techniques. These characteristics are in essence, that a scenario describes a possible future situation and explores while doing so the paths which lead to that outcome (p. 11). They further propose that scenarios are shedding light only on segments of the future and deliberately spare out on some aspects, they are further more constructed in that regard that the underlying developments for those future situations are made up based on more or less probable factors. Accordingly they are based on assumptions of the development of certain trends that can be observed in the respective area already and are, as such trends are extrapolated during the development of a future scenario entirely hypothetical (pp. 11-13).

Jackson (2013, p. 24) defines scenarios subsequently and more from a practical point of view as a vision of distinct quality, that are told as stories and elaborate in those how the future might looks. In order of doing so, they make assumptions of connections and modes of actions.

Especially practical oriented scholars differ between a huge variety of scenario techniques, varying in their complexity, purpose and outcome (Pherson, 2015, p. 5; Jackson, 2013, p. 24; UNIDO, n.d., pp. 69-75). However all of them share a basic methodology (see figure 1).

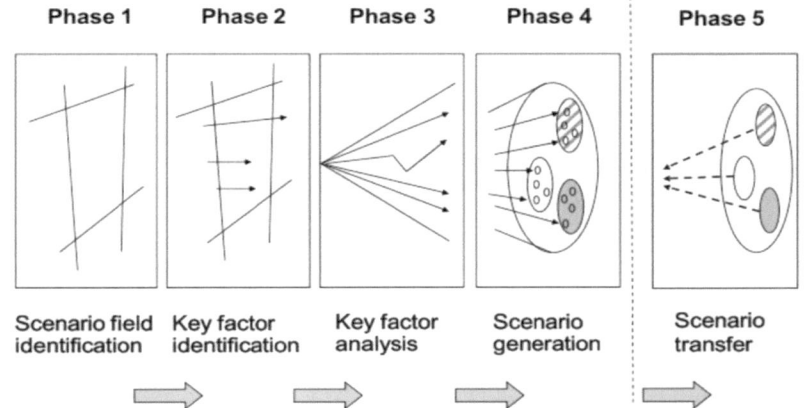

Figure 1: Key process steps of scenario analyses (Source: Kosow and Gassner, 2008, p. 25).

This process basically consists of the identification of a scenario canvas, the derivation of key factors and the elaboration of these factors into scenario stories (Kosow and Gassner, 2008, pp. 25-30), that basically underline one of five main points (Pherson, 2015, p. 9):

- The most credible downside risk,
- The consensus or mainline assessment,
- A new opportunity,
- A new or previously unexamined trend or dynamic
- A scenario the customer will recognize and find credible.

Because of the needed transfer ability to underline these mentioned focal points Popper (2008, p. 72) defines scenarios as a very creative foresight technique.

UNIDO (n.d., p. 69) and Kosow and Gassner (2008, pp. 25-30) define the use of scenarios as:

- Illustrating and communicating features of forecasts and future-relevant analyses (communication function),
- Providing a framework in terms of which views of different aspects of future developments can be integrated and their consistency or otherwise examined (goal setting function).
- Structuring and guiding discussion so that visions, elements of visions, and the assumptions that underpin such visions, can be explicated and elaborated (strategy formation function).

2 Advantages and disadvantages of scenarios

According to Kosow and Gassner (2008, pp. 32-34) scenarios can be divided into either normative or explorative and qualitative and quantitative types, which basically makes, among others, for four different types of scenarios, e.g. explorative qualitative scenarios. The characteristics of these types are shown in figure 2.

	Quantitative	Qualitative
Implementation	When quantitative knowledge – is required – and present – and/or quantification is possible	When qualitative knowledge – is required – or quantitative knowledge is not present – or quantitative knowledge is not present
Topic areas	e.g. demography, economic development	e.g. institutions, culture, politics
Impact on the degree of formalization	Tendency to a high degree of formalization	Tendency to a low degree of formalization
The ideal-typical scenario technique	Modeling methods	Narrative and/or literary techniques
Manner of selecting key factors	Firm definition of a narrowly limited number of factors	Intrinsically sensory observation of details and nuances, possible without a stringent selection of factors
Chronological projection space	Short to medium-term	Medium to long-term

	Explorative	Normative
Procedure	Explores possible future developments with the present as point of departure	Identifies desirable futures or investigates how to arrive at future conditions
Function	Explorative and/or knowledge function	Target-building function and/or strategy development function
Implementation	Study of factors and unpredictabilities, test of possible actions to be taken and/or decision-making processes	Definition and concretization of goals and/or, if appropriate, identification of possible ways to reach a goal
Central question	What? – What if?	How? – How is it to come about? – How do we get there?
Inclusion of probabilities	Possible	Indirect, part of plausible shaping and planning

Figure 2: Characteristics of qualitative vs. quantitative and explorative vs. normative scenarios (Source: Kosow and Gassner, 2008, pp. 32-34).

Mietzner and Regner (2005, p. 233) provide a framework for the basic value assessment of a scenario analysis. The criteria which a scenario should meet to provide according to its assigned use to a foresight exercise are a) Plausibility, as the scenarios have to be able to actually happen, b) Differentiation, as in a structural difference and not only a simple variation of each other, c) Consistency, avoidance of built-in internal inconsistencies, d) Decision-making utility, as a scenario should contribute insights into the future that help to make decisions and finally e) Challenge, as the scenarios should challenge the practitioner's conventional wisdom.

The advantages and disadvantages of scenarios are broadly discussed, especially under the notion of their practical relevance (Jackson, 2013, pp. 24-25). In Addition Mietzner and Regner (2005, pp. 235-236) propose an exhaustive overview of advantages and disadvantages of the use of a scenario technique. The strengths are:

- They describe multiple futures, and directly compare them to each other;
- Scenarios are mind openers and to challenge long-held internal beliefs of an organization; and therefore has the chance to change the corporate culture;

- Using them one can recognize and plan with 'weak signals', discontinuities and disruptions to be better prepared to handle new situations;
- According to their core function they improve the creation of a common language for dealing with strategic issues, starting a strategic conversation within an organization;
- The sharing of mutual aims, opportunities, risks, and strategies within the analyzing team improves coordination and general organizational learning;
- Scenario building is highly adoptable to most of the practioner's current situations.

To the contrary the disadvantages are (ibid.):
- Scenario building is very time consuming;
- Scenarios are highly depended on the selection of suitable experts and information
- A deep initial understanding and knowledge of the actual topic is necessary
- Shifting focus from black and white scenarios or the most appealing scenario during the scenario-building process might be hard but should be forced as it otherwise may corrupt the exercises outcome.

In conclusion it is to state, that scenario building is for the said reasons a very powerful tool not only for foresight studies but also for internal communication and the compression of existing knowledge. However it should be deliberately planned what kind of scenario building process, technique and outcome is expected and accordingly prepared to embrace its full impact.

3 Reflections on our scenario technique application during our foresight study

Within our foresight exercise we used a qualitative explorative foresight in the shape of an alternative future analysis with the use of two key drivers. However this gave us a fairly hard time, as it was quite a challenge to a) gather enough knowledge, b) decide on the actual most important information and c) extrapolate on the key drivers and their development.

We overcame those challenges by intensive discussions and consequent crosschecking of available information and similar studies.

However this foresight technique has done its deeds in such extend as we gained a deep understanding of our chosen topic and came up with satisfying insights and ideas considering the given limitations of our study. For upcoming studies although we propose another way of conducting a scenario analysis more tailored to the actual needs of a study e.g. a formalized approach to make the selection of the key drivers a little bit less subjective (see figure 3).

Scenario techniques / In the scenario process	Scenarios on the basis of trend extrapolation	Formalized scenario techniques	Morphological analysis	Intuitive logics	Normative-narrative scenarios
Phase 1 "Determination of scenario field"	Demarcation of topics and definition of the scenario's purpose				
Phase 2 "Identification of key factors"	Trend observation and trend analysis (incl. operationalization)	Identification and characterization (e.g. via impact analysis)	Definition of "components" of the "morphological field"	Evaluation and selection of factors according to their unpredictability and degree of impact	Collective collation and ordering of relevant factors
Phase 3 "Analysis of key factors"	Timeseries analysis and statistical trend extrapolation (if appropriate: variation of trends via TIA)	Consistency analysis or cross-impact analysis in order to form consistent bundles of characteristics	Systematic definition of "hypotheses" in the Morphologic Box	Overview of the values of central factors per scenario (line-item description)	Scenario workshop (incl. development and elaboration of germinal visions)
Phase 4 "Scenario generation"	"Most probable" scenario/ BAU scenario	(Statistical) selection of raw scenarios, textualization	Combination of "hypothesis" bundles into consistent scenarios (intuitively or systematically), textualization.	Textualization of scenarios on the basis of expressive titles, convincing lines of action and an overview of salient characteristics (see above)	Normative evaluation and narrative condensation into consistent scenarios (feed-back loops)
Advantages (e.g.)	Verifiable calculations, solid grounds for knowledge of the future in the case of "strong" trends (e.g. demography).	Systematic evaluation of factors, formalized consistency checks & probability calculation of bundles of characteristics; transparent for experts.	"Systematic creative technique", with clear visualization & documentation; high level of analysis and synthesis.	Incorporation of implicit and explicit knowledge, integration of decision-makers (extensive follow-up capability), no stringent constraints on the number of factors to be taken into account.	Participation of many actors of many different types: transparent, consensusproducing discourses, no restrictions on the number of factors to be taken into account, focus on constructive options.
Disadvantages (e.g.)	Requirement of comprehensive (quantitative) data (longterm time series); study of a single possible future (instead of alternative futures); suggestive of too much certainty.	Limited number of factors, not transparent for the layman, intuitive and normative elements are swept under the rug, over-formalization at the cost of substance, resource-intensive.	The number of factors is limited, since the technique otherwise becomes impenetrable; the number of participants is also limited; the process of resource-intensive.	A "closed-shop" technique whose quality and legiti-macy are difficult to assess from the outside.	"Wish-scenarios" tend to be especially selective and provocative: they have only limited appropriateness as an "end product"; they are resource-intensive.

Figure 3: overview of different scenario technique approaches (Source: Kosow and Gassner, 2008, pp. 76-77).

References

Jackson, M., 2013. *Practical Foresight Guide – Chapter 3: Methods.* [pdf] shapingtomorrow.com. Available at: https://www.shapingtomorrow.com/media-centre/pf-ch03.pdf [Accessed 18 June 2017].

Kosow, H. and Gassner, R., 2008. Methods of future and scenario analysis: overview, assessment, and selection criteria. *DIE Research Project "Development Policy : Questions for the Future".* Bonn: Deutsches Institut für Entwicklungspolitik.

Mietzner, D. and Reger, G., 2005. Advantages and disadvantages of scenario approaches for strategic foresight. *Int. J. Technology Intelligence and Planning*, 1 (2), pp. 220-239.

Pherson, R. H., 2015. *Strategic Foresight Nine Techniques for Business and Intelligence Analysis.* Reston, Virginia: Globalytica LLC.

Popper, R., 2008. How are foresight methods selected? *Foresight,* 10 (6), pp. 62-89.

UNIDO, n.d. *Foresight Methodologies – Training Module 2.* [pdf] UNITED NATIONS INDUSTRIAL DEVELOPMENT ORGANIZATION. Available at: https://www.tc.cz/files/istec_publications/textbook2revisedcf_1171283006.pdf [Accessed 18 June 2017].

YOUR KNOWLEDGE HAS VALUE

- We will publish your bachelor's and master's thesis, essays and papers

- Your own eBook and book - sold worldwide in all relevant shops

- Earn money with each sale

Upload your text at www.GRIN.com and publish for free